100 facts

Horses
& Ponies

100 facts
Horses & Ponies

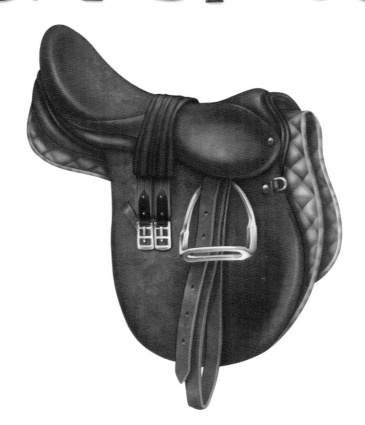

Camilla de la Bedoyere

Consultant: Steve Parker

Miles
Kelly

First published in 2008 by Miles Kelly Publishing Ltd
Harding's Barn, Bardfield End Green, Thaxted, Essex, CM6 3PX

Copyright © Miles Kelly Publishing Ltd 2003

This edition printed in 2016

8 10 12 14 15 13 11 9

Publishing Director Belinda Gallagher
Creative Director Jo Cowan
Editor Rosalind Neave
Editorial Assistant Carly Blake
Volume Designer Elaine Wilkinson
Cover Designer Simon Lee
Picture Researcher Laura Faulder
Reprographics Stephan Davis, Thom Allaway,
Anthony Cambray, Liberty Newton
Production Elizabeth Collins, Caroline Kelly
Archive Manager Jennifer Cozens
Assets Lorraine King

ISBN 978-1-78617-013-2

Printed in China

British Library Cataloguing-in-Publication Data
A catalogue record for this book is available from the British Library

ACKNOWLEDGEMENTS
The publishers would like to thank the following artists
who have contributed to this book:

Mark Davis (Mackerel)/Peter Dennis (Linda Rogers Associates)/
Mike Foster(Maltings Partnership)/Terry Gabbey/
Lindsay Graham (Linden Artists)/Richard Hook (Linden Artists)/
Andrea Morandi/Eric Rowe (Linden Artists)/Rudi Vizi/
Mike White (Temple Rogers)
Cartoons by Mark Davis at Mackerel

All other artworks come from Miles Kelly Archives

The publishers would like to thank the following sources
for the use of their photographs:
Cover: David Chapman/Photoshot.com, Page 14 photolibrary, P37 TopFoto.co.uk

All other photographs from:
Castrol, CMCD, Corbis, Corel, digitalSTOCK, digitalvision, Flat Earth, Hemera,
ILN, John Foxx, PhotoAlto, PhotoDisc, PhotoEssentials, PhotoPro, Stockbyte

Every effort has been made to acknowledge the source and copyright holder of each picture.
Miles Kelly Publishing apologises for any unintentional errors or omissions.

Made with paper from a sustainable forest

www.mileskelly.net
info@mileskelly.net

Contents

Wild and wonderful

1 Strong, elegant and patient – horses have been loyal companions to humans for thousands of years. People have used horses to help them pull loads, plough fields and fight wars – without the help of horses, the story of human history would be very different. Today many people still rely on horses, ponies, donkeys and mules for transport. When they are free to gallop in a field, or live in the wild, we can truly appreciate the beauty and energy of these magnificent animals.

► All horses, wild or tame, enjoy the thrill of galloping at speed. They are sociable animals and prefer to live in groups, or herds.

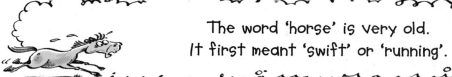

The word 'horse' is very old.
It first meant 'swift' or 'running'.

Meet the family

2 Horses, ponies, zebras and asses all belong to the same animal family – the **equids.** All members of this family have a single toe on each foot and are called 'odd-toed' animals (unlike cows and deer, which have two toes on each foot). Like other animals with fur, horses are mammals and they give birth to live young, which they feed with milk.

▲ Zebras are easily recognized by their stripy coats. These wild equids live in Africa.

3 Ponies are smaller than horses. Although horses and ponies are the same type of animal, they are different sizes. Horses are measured in 'hands', not centimetres, and a pony is a horse that is less than 14.2 hands (or 148 centimetres) tall. Ponies also have wider bodies and shorter legs than horses.

▶ A horse's height is measured from its feet to the top of its shoulders, which are known as 'withers' (see page 11).

4 Equids live all over the world. Wild equids, such as zebras, live on grasslands where they can graze all day on plants. Horses that live and work with humans can be found almost everywhere across the world, and these are known as domestic horses.

5 Equids have manes of long hair on their heads and necks and thick, tufted tails. Their long legs, deep chests and powerful muscles allow them to run a long way at great speed without getting tired.

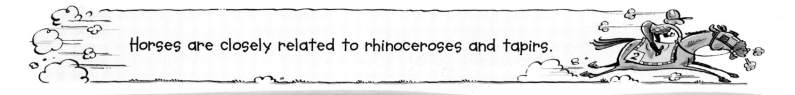
MEASURE IN HANDS

Normally we use centimetres and metres as units of measurement, but you can use anything you like – even your hands.

Measure the height of a table using your hands. Then ask an adult to measure it as well. Did you get the same measurement? If not, why not?

6 Wild horses live in large groups called herds. All horses, wild or domestic (tame), are very loyal to one another and can form close bonds with other animals, including humans. Since it is natural for horses to have company, domestic horses should always be kept together, or with other animals such as sheep and cows.

7 Horses are intelligent animals. They can communicate with each other by whinnying or braying, but, like many other animals, horses also sniff and smell one another to communicate. They also enjoy nuzzling and grooming each other's fur.

▼ In a herd, horses who get on well with each other will groom and nuzzle one another.

9

Inside out

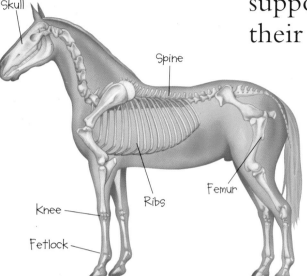

▼ The features of a horse's skeleton, including extended leg bones and a rigid spine, allow it to run at speed for great distances.

Skull

Spine

Femur

Ribs

Knee

Fetlock

8 **Horses have a bony framework called a skeleton.** The skeleton supports their bodies and protects their organs. The skull protects the brain, and the ribs protect the lungs and heart. Bones are made from a hard material called calcium, but are full of tiny holes, which make them lightweight.

9 **Domestic horses all belong to the same species, which means that they can mate with one another.** Within the horse species there are lots of different types of horse, and these are called breeds. Breeds of horse differ in their appearance and in their personalities. A carthorse, for example, might have strong bones and a muscular body that is suited to pulling heavy loads, whereas a racehorse needs long legs and slender bones to run very fast.

Croup

Dock

Tail

Hock

Stifle

Thigh

Fetlock

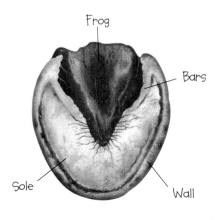

Frog

Bars

Sole

Wall

▲ A horseshoe is nailed to the 'wall' of a hoof.

10 **All equids have hooves, which are made from keratin.** Keratin is the same material that is found in fingernails, hair, fur and claws. Hoof edges can be trimmed without causing any pain to the horse. Domestic horses can be prone to having sore and damaged feet, because they often walk and run on hard, paved surfaces. It is important that their hooves are well looked after.

11 The parts of a horse's body that you can see are called 'the points of a horse'. Each point is given a special name and people who work with horses and ponies, or ride them, have to learn these names.

▼ Recognized terms or 'points' are used to pinpoint particular areas of a horse's body.

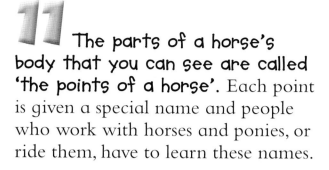

Poll

Crest

Ear

Withers

Back

Nostril

Muzzle

Shoulder

Breast

Forearm

Knee

Cannon bone

Fetlock

Hoof

I DON'T BELIEVE IT!

It takes from nine months to one year for a horse to grow a completely new hoof. When a horse gallops, all of its weight is supported by just one slender hoof at a time.

12 A person who looks after hooves and makes horseshoes is called a farrier. The farrier cleans and trims the hoof, before attaching the iron shoe to the hoof by hammering long nails through the shoe and through the edge of the hoof wall. This doesn't hurt the horse at all.

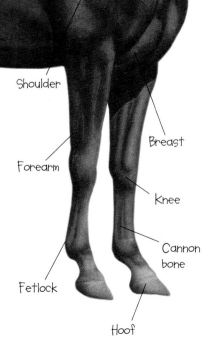

▶ Metal horseshoes are heated and hammered into shape before fitting.

Colours and markings

Star

Stripe

White face

Blaze

Snip

13 **The fur of horses and ponies comes in a wide range of colours.** The most common are bay (red-brown), chestnut (red-gold), grey (which can be almost white to dark grey), brown (dark bay) and black. There are also many other colour variations, such as dun (sandy brown), bright bay (light bay) and liver chestnut (dark chestnut).

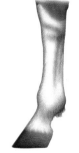
Over knee (stocking)

Mid-cannon

Fetlock

14 **Horses often have markings on their lower legs.** These are called socks. White socks that extend above the knee are called stockings. Horses may have white marks elsewhere on their bodies – a white mark on the belly is called a 'flesh mark'.

Half-pastern (sock)

Crown

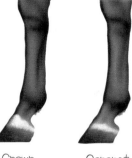
Coronet

▲ White leg markings are described using the points of anatomy that the white hair covers.

15 **White patches of fur on a horse's face are often used to help identify a horse.** A 'stripe' is a narrow band of white that runs down the face, a 'blaze' is a broad band, a 'star' is a white mark on the forehead and a 'snip' is a patch of white between the horse's nostrils.

◄ A full description of a horse would include natural marks.

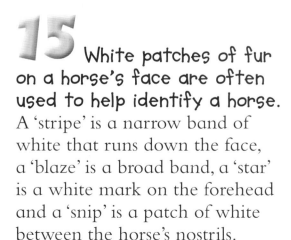
ODD ONE OUT!
Find the animal that has neither stripes nor spots:

1. Cheetah 2. Hover fly
3. Walrus 4. Coral snake
5. Song thrush

Answer: 3. Walrus

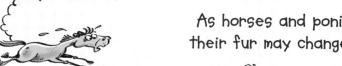

16 Some wild equids have stripes or dark marks along their spines. Zebras are the most famous of all striped animals, but other wild equids sometimes have stripy legs, or a stripe of black fur running from the mane to the tail. This darker stripe is called an 'eel stripe'.

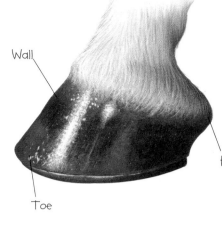

Wall

Heel

Toe

▲ A horse's hooves may be dark, light, plain or striped.

18 Horses' hooves can also be different colours. A horse with dark legs is likely to also have dark hooves. Pale horses, or those with white socks, often have hooves that are a pale colour – usually cream. Dark hooves are called 'blue' and pale hooves are called 'white'.

17 Some breeds of horse have large patches of different colours on their coats. These horses are called 'part-coloured'. Horses with patches of white and black fur are called 'piebald'. Horses with large patches of white and any other colour, apart from black, on their coats are called 'skewbald'.

► Horses that are referred to as 'piebald' usually have large, irregular patches of white and black hairs on their coat. Pinto horses are popular piebalds in the United States.

Hold your horses!

▼ Wild horses often run, or gallop, when they are scared. A stallion usually leads the way.

19 **A horse's body is packed with muscles.** These help it to run fast, jump and leap, and pull heavy loads. The world's fastest wild equid is the onager – an ass that can reach an incredible top speed of 78 kilometres an hour!

20 **The way in which a horse moves is called the 'gait' or 'pace'.** In the wild, horses move at their own pace and only have two gaits, walking slowly as they graze and galloping when they are frightened. Domestic horses are trained to perform at least four different gaits.

Walk

Trot

21

The 'walk' is the slowest gait. It has a four-beat rhythm. The horse places its left foreleg forwards, then its right hind (back) leg, followed by its right foreleg and then its left hind leg. The 'trot' is the next fastest gait and it has a two-beat rhythm. As the horse moves, two legs (for example, the left foreleg and the right hind leg) touch the ground at the same time, while the other two legs (the right foreleg and the left hind leg) are in the air.

22

The canter and gallop are the fastest two gaits. When a horse canters it has a three-beat rhythm, and there is a moment when all four of the horse's feet are off the ground. Galloping is the most exciting of the gaits. It is similar to the canter, but faster and with longer strides. Each foot strikes the ground separately. The moment when all four feet are in the air at the same time is called the suspension.

I DON'T BELIEVE IT!

At full gallop, Thoroughbred racehorses can reach speeds of over 60 kilometres an hour, even with riders on their backs.

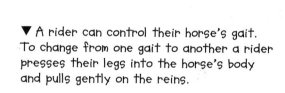

▼ A rider can control their horse's gait. To change from one gait to another a rider presses their legs into the horse's body and pulls gently on the reins.

Canter

Gallop

Colts and fillies

23 **Only a few hours after they are born, baby horses (foals) are able to stand up and walk around.** Like the young of other hoofed animals, foals born in the wild are at risk of being hunted and caught by predators. For this reason, foals spend a long time – about 11 months – developing inside their mothers so they are ready to move and feed soon after they are born.

24 **Mares – female horses – usually give birth to just one foal at a time.** When a foal is born it rests for a few minutes, but soon attempts to stand and feed from its mother. The mare licks her newborn clean. She sniffs her foal to get used to its smell and the mother and foal whinny to one another, learning the sounds of each other's voices.

▶ In the first weeks of its life a foal stays next to its mother at all times. Mares can even sleep standing up, and are easily wakened if their youngster needs protection or reassurance.

25

Foals stay close to their mothers for the first two months of their lives. After this time the foals become braver and more adventurous, and will move away to investigate other members of the herd. Soon after this they begin to groom and play with other horses. When a young horse is between 12 and 24 months old, it is called a yearling. A female yearling is known as a filly, and a male yearling is known as a colt.

26

An expert can tell how old a horse is by looking at its teeth. The front, cutting, teeth are incisors and they are used to slice grass and other tender plants. As a horse ages, its incisors change from an oval shape to round, then become triangular and flattened. By examining the length and shape of a horse's teeth, it is possible to estimate its age.

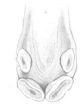

Up to 6 months

At 5 years

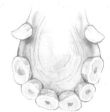

At 15 years

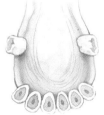

At 25 years

WHAT TYPE OF ANIMAL AM I?

The young of animals are often given special names, like foal or calf. Use a dictionary to find out what type of animals these other youngsters are:

1. Eaglet 2. Gosling
3. Leveret 4. Maggot

Answers: 1. Eagle 2. Goose 3. Hare 4. Fly

▲ A horse's teeth change as it gets older. Teeth get gradually worn down with use and become more triangular in shape. Their surface markings also change.

Sensitive and smart

27 Horses have better senses of sight, hearing and smell than humans. Long ago the grasslands of the world were home to thousands of herds of equids, such as horses, zebra and asses. These grazing animals made good meals for predators. In order to keep themselves safe, horses needed to have highly developed senses of hearing, sight and smell so that they could detect any lurking predators.

▲ Grooming, stroking and talking all help to build a special friendship between horse and rider.

28 Domestic horses and ponies like and need company. They can often become very close to the people who care for them, or ride them. Talking to horses may feel silly, but it isn't. They are such intelligent animals that they quickly begin to recognize voices, and can learn to understand simple words, such as 'no', 'stop' and 'go'.

29 A horse's eye is twice as large as a human's eye, and is even bigger than an elephant's eye. Horses' eyes are positioned on the side of their heads, which means they can see in almost every direction. That's helpful when you always need to be on the look-out for a hungry predator.

I DON'T BELIEVE IT!

Horses have such good hearing that they have been known to sense earthquakes before humans are aware of them.

30

Horses are able to recognize friends, both human and animal, by smell alone. Animals that live in groups have to be able to communicate with each other, and horses are no exception. Horses use the position of their ears to communicate their feelings – when their ears point backwards, horses are showing that they are scared or anxious.

31

A herd of wild horses includes only one adult male, called a stallion. There are normally only about seven horses in a herd – one stallion with his mares and foals. The stallion protects his family and fights any other males that come too close to the herd.

▼ Stallions start to fight when they are four to five years old. They will rear up and kick their rivals, and aim bites at the throat, neck, ears or tail.

19

Hungry as a horse!

32 **Wild horses can spend between 16 and 20 hours a day feeding.** The main bulk of their food is grass, which is difficult to digest. This means that horses need to eat a lot to get the energy that they need. Horses even eat during the night because they can see well in the dark and they only need a small amount of sleep. They will often nap for just a few minutes at a time, while still on their feet.

▶ Different types of teeth are used in eating. A horse's incisors cut and pull up plants. Its molars and premolars grind and mash the food. The surface of the teeth is worn down by about 3 millimetres every year.

34 **Horses are fussy eaters.** They will spend time looking for a good patch of plants before they settle down to graze. Although they like grass, horses enjoy other plants such as cocksfoot, wild white clover, dandelions and chicory. They use their flexible top lips to grab the plant, then bite off a clump with their incisor teeth.

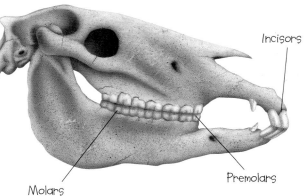

Incisors

Premolars

Molars

33 **Horses can't bring up food, so if they eat something poisonous it can kill them.** Horses can poison themselves with the natural vegetation found in their fields, or in the trees and hedges surrounding their paddocks. Horses learn to avoid plants that taste bad, or cause them stomach pain, but not all dangerous plants have these obvious effects. Domestic horses and ponies should be kept in fields from which poisonous plants such as foxglove, yew, bracken, buttercups, laurel and laburnum have been removed.

Oak

◀▶ Ragwort, oak leaves and acorns are dangerous to horses. These plants should be removed from a horse's field.

Ragwort

35 Some domestic horses are given their food, so they do not have to graze all day. Their normal diet of grass and fresh plants is replaced with hay and other food. Horses have small stomachs, so they need to be given lots of small meals, rather than a few large ones. Hay is dry grass, so although horses enjoy it, they have to be given plenty of fresh water to help them digest it easily.

36 Removing a horse's or pony's droppings is called 'mucking out'. Horses produce lots of waste – manure – every day and clearing this away is an important job for anyone who owns a horse or pony. Manure is useful stuff – it can be left to rot, and then used in gardens or farms to put goodness back into the soil.

▼ Food such as oats, barley, sugar beet and bran are known as 'hard feed'. They may be mixed with chopped hay and straw and given to a horse or pony.

CHOOSE THE CORRECT WORD

1. Are animals that are active at night nocturnal or nautical?
2. Are rotting plants or manure called compost or comical?
3. Is tomahawk or toxin another name for poison?

Answers: 1. Nocturnal 2. Compost 3. Toxin

Habitats and homes

37 The first equids are thought to have lived in the area we now call America, when it was joined to other continents. A continent is a big region of land, such as Africa or North America, and long ago the continents were connected. From America, horses were able to spread to Europe, Asia and Africa.

38 After the last ice age, which ended about 10,000 years ago, millions of wild horses roamed the grasslands of Europe and Asia. They probably lived in herds, travelling great distances in search of food and water. The numbers of horses gradually decreased as the climate changed. Horses were also hunted by people, who used them for food and fur.

▼ Zebras now live in Africa but, like other equids, they originally came from North America.

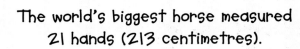

39 Domestic horses are found all over the world. There are very few equids living in the wild now, but there are millions of domesticated horses that live or work with people who depend on them for transport or pulling loads.

▶ Most types of horses are domestic, but some wild horses still roam free.

40 The place where an animal lives is called its habitat. Wild horses are usually well-suited to their habitat. Those that live in cold areas may have very thick fur. The tarpan was an ancient type of horse with a coat that turned white during the snowy winter weather of its north European home.

41 Wild asses are found in western Asia and the Middle East. Asses are the ancestors of modern donkeys, which first lived in North Africa. Since then, donkeys have spread to other parts of the world, and are common in Europe.

▼ The ancestors of the shire horse had to develop bulky bodies to help them survive the cold winters of northern Europe.

I DON'T BELIEVE IT!

About 10,000 years ago horses became extinct (died out) in the Americas. They were reintroduced by Spanish travellers about 500 years ago.

The first horses

Hyracotherium
50 million
years ago

Mesohippus
36 million years
ago

Parahippus
24 million
years ago

42 The very first horse—like animal is thought to have lived about 50 million years ago. It is called *Hyracotherium*. By looking at its remains and teeth, scientists have decided that *Hyracotherium* probably lived on a diet of leaves. It had four toes on its front feet and three toes on its hind feet.

▼ The horse has adapted to changing conditions over millions of years. By the time of *Equus*, horses had grown larger, their necks were longer and their extra toes had disappeared.

Merychippus
17 million years ago

Pliohippus
5 million years ago

Equus
1.5 million years ago

43 It is believed that *Hyracotherium* is the ancestor of modern horses. Over millions of years animals can change so that they are better suited to the environment in which they live. This process is called evolution.

◄ Palaeontologists are scientists who study ancient animal remains.

MAKE A FAMILY TREE

You probably have some ancient relatives too! Look through old photograph albums and talk to your parents and grandparents to find out about members of your family. See how many years back you can trace. Do you look similar to any of your relatives?

44 There are only ten species of equids, but hundreds of different breeds of domestic horse. A species of animal includes any members of a group that can mate with one another to produce healthy young that are the same, or very similar. Breeds are different types, or varieties, of animals in one species.

45 Gradually, *Hyracotherium* evolved so that it could survive in a changing world. By 36 million years ago this ancient creature had disappeared, but a different horse-like animal lived – *Mesohippus*. It was the size of a sheep and had three toes on each foot, a long neck and a slender face.

▼ Unlike modern horses, who prefer to live on open grasslands and plains, *Hyracotherium* was a forest dweller.

25

Asses, donkeys and mules

46 An ass is a wild horse that is sure—footed and able to survive in very harsh conditions. Asses are shorter than most members of the horse family, and they are famous for their ability to live in places where there is little food or water. Wild asses are found mainly in Africa and Asia, where rain rarely falls and the ground is stony. Asses can survive on a diet of dry grass and thorny shrubs and bushes.

47 Long before farmers had tractors, they used animals to work in their fields. Onagers, which are a type of ass, were probably the first animals that were used to pull ploughs and carts. They are extremely fast runners, strong and reliable. Today, these gentle creatures are in danger of extinction.

48 Przewalski's wild horse looks similar to an ass, with its short stocky body. The last free Przewalski's horse was seen in the 1970s, in Mongolia. Today, these unusual beasts are mostly kept in zoos or parks, but a small herd has now been put back into the wild.

◄ Przewalski's horse is heavily built. It has a large head, thick neck and short legs.

A female donkey is called a jenny
and a male is called a jackass!

► Donkeys and mules have often been used to carry heavy loads. This mule train, under attack, is carrying treasure.

49 **Donkeys are asses that have been domesticated.** They are used to carry people or goods, and for farming. They are very strong and can live in harsh habitats, often walking for many miles in the heat with little food or water.

▼ Donkeys are popular with tourists at the seaside, where they carry children down the beach.

MATING GAME
When two different species of animals are mated, their youngster (like a mule) is called a 'hybrid'. Can you guess the parents of these hybrids?

1. Geep 2. Tigon
3. Wholphin

Answers: 1. Goat and sheep
2. Tiger and lion 3. Whale and dolphin

50 **If a female horse mates with a male donkey, the foal is called a mule.** Mules combine the horse's strength with the donkey's ability to keep working in difficult conditions. If a male horse mates with a female donkey, the foal is called a hinny. Mules and hinnies are sterile, which means that they cannot have any foals themselves.

On the African plains

51 Zebras are wild horses that have startling patterns of black-and-white striped fur. They are found in Africa, where they live on the huge grasslands known as the savannah, along with other grazing or browsing creatures such as giraffes, wildebeests and antelopes.

52 There are three types, or species, of zebra – Grevy's, mountain and Burchell's. A Grevy's zebra lives further north than the other two species. It is the tallest of the three types and has very thin stripes, particularly on its face. The mountain zebra has a dark muzzle and thick black stripes on its rump. It is in danger of becoming extinct. The most common of the three types is Burchell's zebra.

Grevy's zebra

Burchell's zebra

Mountain zebra

▲ Zebra types can be identified by the pattern of stripes on their fur.

▼ The common, or Burchell's, zebra has broad horizontal stripes that extend under the belly.

53 **No one knows for sure why zebras have stripes.** It was thought that the patterns might confuse predators. Or it may be for purposes of identification – each zebra has a unique pattern of stripes, and a zebra can recognize another member of its herd just by its pattern of stripes.

54 **There was a fourth type of zebra – the quagga – but it is now extinct.** Quaggas lived in southern Africa, in herds of up to a hundred individuals. Like other zebras, they lived on grasslands and spent most of their day grazing. They were ruthlessly hunted by European settlers and the last one died in 1883.

Horse tales

60 For thousands of years, horses have appeared in art, songs and stories. One of the most famous horse stories is *Black Beauty* – a tale about a noble horse, written by Anna Sewell and first published in 1877. The story is written from the viewpoint of the horse. The book was hugely popular, particularly with people who lived and worked with horses.

I DON'T BELIEVE IT!

For a while after his death, people believed that the Roman Emperor Caligula had loved his horse so much that he had dressed it in purple robes and built it a house!

▼ *Black Beauty* was set in Victorian times. It tells of the days when horses worked extremely hard and were often very badly treated.

Grevy's zebra

Burchell's zebra

Mountain zebra

▲ Zebra types can be identified by the pattern of stripes on their fur.

▼ The common, or Burchell's, zebra has broad horizontal stripes that extend under the belly.

53 **No one knows for sure why zebras have stripes.** It was thought that the patterns might confuse predators. Or it may be for purposes of identification – each zebra has a unique pattern of stripes, and a zebra can recognize another member of its herd just by its pattern of stripes.

54 **There was a fourth type of zebra – the quagga – but it is now extinct.** Quaggas lived in southern Africa, in herds of up to a hundred individuals. Like other zebras, they lived on grasslands and spent most of their day grazing. They were ruthlessly hunted by European settlers and the last one died in 1883.

55 No one knows for sure when horses and ponies were first used by people for riding, pulling or carrying things. However, there are pictures of men on horseback that are more than 4000 years old! Since ancient times, horses, ponies, asses and donkeys have helped humans explore their world.

▼ This horse–drawn machine, called a 'seed drill', dropped seeds in to a ploughed field and helped make farming more efficient.

56 For thousands of years, horses went to war. In ancient Persia (now Iran) and Rome, horses pulled chariots, which took soldiers wielding swords and spears into battle, or to entertain crowds in large arenas.

◄ In the Middle Ages, kings and knights led their armies to war on horses chosen for their strength and obedience.

57 Horses have been used in farming and for carrying or pulling heavy weights. The strongest members of the horse family have been chosen by farmers to help them move carts weighed down with crops, or to plough fields and carry water. In most modern countries, machinery has replaced horses, but across the world many people still rely on their horses to help them grow their crops.

58

The United States of America was explored by settlers with horses. The USA covers a vast area. Without horses and mules it would have been very difficult for European travellers to make their way across the huge continent. Hundreds of horse-drawn wagons formed a winding trail as they travelled west to set up new towns and farming communities.

▶ Annie Oakley was an American rodeo star and sharp shooter.

EXPLORE!

Discover more about an area near you and arrange a trip there with family or friends.
You will need:
map food drinks
Choose a place you have never visited before, so like a real explorer, you'll see everything for the first time. Decide how you will travel there, and plan carefully. Make sure you take an adult with you when you go.

59

A thousand years ago, medieval soldiers took part in tournaments on horseback. They sat astride their large and powerful horses, which had to carry their riders and heavy metal armour too, as they jousted with one another to prove their courage and strength.

Horse tales

60 **For thousands of years, horses have appeared in art, songs and stories.** One of the most famous horse stories is *Black Beauty* – a tale about a noble horse, written by Anna Sewell and first published in 1877. The story is written from the viewpoint of the horse. The book was hugely popular, particularly with people who lived and worked with horses.

▼ *Black Beauty* was set in Victorian times. It tells of the days when horses worked extremely hard and were often very badly treated.

61 Magical horses appear in the *Lord of the Rings* stories, written by J.R.R. Tolkien. The tales describe a tribe of horses called the Mearas. Shadowfax is the elegant and intelligent Chief of the Mearas, and he comes to the aid of Gandalf in the wizard's heroic fight against evil.

▶ Bellerophon and his winged horse Pegasus were mythical heroes of Greek legends.

62 According to an ancient story, a huge wooden horse was used by the Greeks to invade the city of Troy. Greek soldiers built the huge model and concealed themselves inside it. The curious Trojans, believing it to be a gift, hauled the horse inside their city's walls. While the kingdom slept, the Greeks crept out and slaughtered them.

63 Unicorns appear in stories, or fables, from ancient India, China, the Middle East and Greece. It was believed that they had magical properties. These mythological creatures were described as white horses with blue eyes and a horn growing out of their foreheads, but from this description it is possible that the ancient storytellers were actually describing rhinoceroses!

▶ In Norse mythology, Odin's steed Sleipnir was considered to be the greatest of all horses.

64 Many ancient myths feature magical horses. Pegasus was a stallion with white wings in ancient Greek mythology. A Greek legend tells how Bellerophon tamed Pegasus with the help of the goddess Athene. Odin, the Viking god of war, was said to have ridden an eight-legged horse, called Sleipnir.

Wild ponies

65 Ponies are usually smaller than horses, with wider bodies and shorter legs. They often come from areas of the world where they have had to struggle to survive, so they show great stamina. Ponies are usually sure-footed, which means that they can easily get about on steep hillsides and rocky plains. Wild ponies have often lost their habitats to humans, but some breeds still live on the moors and grasslands of the world.

▲ The Highland is the largest of the Scottish breeds and can survive where food is scarce.

66 Connemara ponies originally came from Ireland, but they are now bred throughout Europe. Connemaras have been bred with Arab and Thoroughbred horses, and they have inherited speed and good jumping ability from these famous horse breeds. Connemaras are strong, sturdy and intelligent. They make good competition horses and are popular with both adults and children.

TRUE OR FALSE?
1. Ponies can suffer from sunburn.
2. Some horses are allergic to dust.
3. Little bugs, called mites, can live in ponies' ears, making them itchy.

Answers: All are true

▶ Wild Connemara ponies have lived on the moors of western Ireland since the 16th century.

67 Tiny Shetland ponies first arrived in Scotland about 10,000 years ago, from Scandinavia. They live in harsh conditions, which has led to the breed developing great strength. Shetland ponies are measured in inches, not hands, and they stand up to 40 inches (102 centimetres) tall. For their size, Shetlands are probably the strongest of all horse and pony breeds.

▼ Shetland ponies have thick fur and manes to protect them from the cold. They have large noses and nostrils so they can warm the air before it reaches their lungs.

68 New Forest ponies have been living wild for about a thousand years. They live in protected woodlands and heaths of Hampshire in southern England. The ponies can graze and mate freely. This type of pony can also be tamed and used in riding stables, where it is particularly popular with children.

69 Two of the most famous breeds of wild pony are the Dartmoor and Exmoor. These sturdy ponies can survive the difficult conditions found on the moors – they have to be tough enough to cope with rain, snow, biting winds and the poor grazing. The Exmoor is one of the oldest breeds in the world, and dates back as far as the last ice age – 10,000 years ago! Tame Dartmoor ponies are often used for riding lessons, as they are strong and they jump well.

Ponies as pets

70 In the past, ponies were used to haul carts and work on farms, but today they are most often kept as pets. Children who want to learn how to ride usually have their first lessons on a pony. Ponies are good-natured animals. They are reliable and patient, so boys and girls can often form very close friendships with them.

71 Fell ponies are famous for their ability to work very hard. They were once used in mines and on farms, and could travel hundreds of kilometres in one week, pulling carts. Fell ponies are only 14 hands (142 centimetres) high, but they are strong enough to carry adults and they are popular ponies for children.

◄ Fell ponies are usually black or dark brown, occasionally with small white markings. Their bodies are deep, their legs are short and strong and they have long, thick tails.

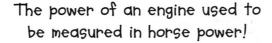

▲ Falabella horses are so small they can even be
dwarfed by a dog! Falabellas have large heads,
slender legs and thick manes and tails.

I DON'T BELIEVE IT!

Pit ponies used to work
below ground, in mines, and
were often looked after by
children who also worked there.
The ponies were often better
fed and cared
for than the
children
were.

72 **The little Falabella is the smallest of all the horse breeds.**
It is a very new type of horse, which
has been created by the Falabella
family of Argentina, who mated
Shetland ponies with Thoroughbred
horses. A Falabella only stands about
7 hands (71 centimetres) tall, but it is
often called a miniature horse
rather than a pony because of its
horse-like character and
body shape. Falabellas are
too small to be ridden, but
they are popular as pets.
Falabella foals are
usually only 4 hands
(41 centimetres) tall.

73 **Welsh mountain ponies make excellent riding ponies.** They are divided
into four different types – Section A, B, C
and D. Welsh Section A ponies come from the
Welsh mountains. Section B, C and D ponies
have been developed by breeding Section A
ponies with other types of horse or pony.
They are often used for jumping or driving.

▶ Welsh cobs make good
driving ponies – this
means they can be used
for pulling a cart or trap.

Hotblood horses

74 Horse breeds are divided into three main groups, called hotbloods, warmbloods and coldbloods. Hotbloods are ancient and very pure breeds that originally came from North Africa and the Middle East. They are very elegant and fast runners. Coldbloods come from northern Europe and they are large, heavy, strong horses. Warmbloods were developed by mating hotbloods with coldbloods.

75 The most famous of all hotbloods is the Arab. These lively and speedy horses first lived in the desert regions of the Middle East. They are said to be the oldest domestic horse breed in the world, as well as the most beautiful. Arabs are small, but they are famous for their stamina. Like Thoroughbreds and Akhal-Tekés, Arabs are a high-spirited breed and are not usually considered suitable horses for young or inexperienced riders.

76 Although horses come in all sorts of shapes and sizes, they are divided into breeds. Within each breed, the horses are similar in personality and appearance. By mating a horse from one breed with a horse of another breed, people (called breeders) have been able to create new and different types of horse, such as warmbloods.

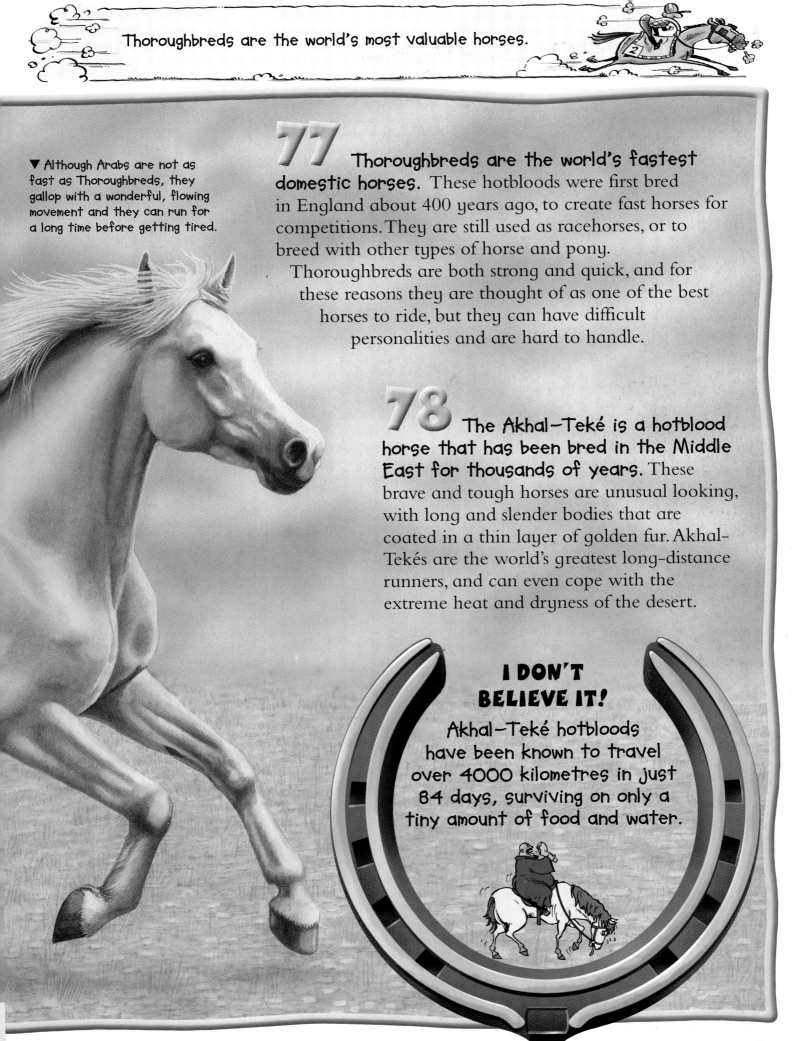

▼ Although Arabs are not as fast as Thoroughbreds, they gallop with a wonderful, flowing movement and they can run for a long time before getting tired.

77 **Thoroughbreds are the world's fastest domestic horses.** These hotbloods were first bred in England about 400 years ago, to create fast horses for competitions. They are still used as racehorses, or to breed with other types of horse and pony. Thoroughbreds are both strong and quick, and for these reasons they are thought of as one of the best horses to ride, but they can have difficult personalities and are hard to handle.

78 **The Akhal-Teké is a hotblood horse that has been bred in the Middle East for thousands of years.** These brave and tough horses are unusual looking, with long and slender bodies that are coated in a thin layer of golden fur. Akhal-Tekés are the world's greatest long-distance runners, and can even cope with the extreme heat and dryness of the desert.

I DON'T BELIEVE IT!

Akhal-Teké hotbloods have been known to travel over 4000 kilometres in just 84 days, surviving on only a tiny amount of food and water.

39

Warmblood horses

79 **Most horse breeds of the world are warmbloods.** Despite their name, the blood of warmbloods is exactly the same temperature as that of hotbloods and coldbloods! The name refers to where different types of horses come from. Hotbloods first came from desert areas, while coldbloods came from cold countries of the north – and warmbloods are a mixture of both!

▼ A Lipizzaner stallion performs a movement called the 'levade'.

▼ Quarter horses have become famous for being those ridden by cowboys when they tend their cattle. They were bred for riding and farm work.

80 **The Quarter horse is said to be the most popular horse in the world.** It works hard, but it also has a calm and patient personality. Quarter horses were first bred in the USA, about 350 years ago. They combine great strength with agility – they can stop, start and change direction very quickly.

81 **The Spanish Riding School of Vienna is known throughout the world for the athletic tricks performed by its Lipizzaner horses.** These grey warmbloods have Spanish ancestors (which is how the Riding School got its name) and they are trained to perform special movements, such as jumps and kicks. The movements are said to be based on medieval tricks of war that were used to evade enemy soldiers. It takes many years to train just one horse.

82 **Camargue horses have been called the 'wild white horses of the sea'.** These beautiful white warmbloods come from the bleak and windswept Rhône region of southern France. As a result, they are extremely tough. It is thought that they are related to the primitive horses that appear in French cave drawings, which are about 17,000 years old. There are herds of wild Camargue horses, but domesticated ones are used by local cowboys to round up wild black bulls.

MAKE TASTY HORSESHOES

You will need:
packet of bread mix

1. Follow the instructions carefully to mix the dough and knead it.
2. Make small balls that you can then mould into strips and shape into horseshoes.
3. Leave the dough to rise, then sprinkle with sesame seeds and bake in the oven. Eat the horseshoes with butter and jam while they are still warm.

83 **One of the most unusual–looking warmbloods is the Appaloosa.** It is known for its strikingly patterned coat, which can be a variety of different colours. This American breed got its name from the Palouse River in the USA. It was bred during the 18th century by a Native American tribe, who wanted to create strong and agile working horses.

▶ There are five Appaloosa coat patterns: marble, blanket, leopard, snowflake and frost. Shown here are blanket (white quarters and loins, sometimes with dark spots) and frost (dark background with white speckles).

Coldblood horses

84 Coldblood horses come from the cooler regions of the world, and they are the largest and strongest of all horse types. Coldbloods have been bred for their immense power, and they have been used to pull heavy loads for hundreds of years, particularly on farms. They have wide backs, muscle-packed bodies and thick, short legs. They usually have very calm, docile natures.

▼ Heavy horses carried medieval knights into war. They are the ancestors of breeds such as the Shire horse (in Britain) and the Percheron (in France).

85 Coldbloods are also known as 'heavy' or 'draught' horses. Before trains and motor vehicles were invented, these horses worked hard as they ploughed fields, pulled boats along canals or hauled carts. In medieval times, these heavyweights were needed to help carry knights to fields of war.

86 Heavy horses are often dressed up and shown in competitions. The owners of these magnificent creatures often travel to country shows and fairs where they give demonstrations to show their horses' strength and power. The horses' manes are braided and plaited, and they are decorated with brasses and gleaming harnesses.

87 The Shire is often called the greatest of all draught horses. It is tall, strong and very gentle. It gets its name from the English counties of Derbyshire, Lincolnshire, Staffordshire and Leicestershire, where it was first bred. Shire horses carried English Medieval knights into battle, and also worked on farms and in cities.

I DON'T BELIEVE IT!

Horses rarely live to be older than 30 years, but an English draught horse, called Old Billy, is said to have made it to the grand age of 62!

88 Suffolk Punches are coldbloods that are all related to a single male horse, which was born in 1768. Suffolks were bred to work on farms but their distinctive chestnut colour makes them a popular breed at shows and competitions.

▲ Shire horses can stand more than 18 hands (180 centimetres) tall and are probably the largest heavy horses. They are usually black, bay, brown or grey in colour, and their legs often have long white stockings. Most heavy horses have wispy fur, called feathers, around their hooves.

Horses for courses

89 Horses and ponies have to learn how to be ridden, or how to pull a cart, wagon or trap. Horses begin this training while they are still young foals. Teaching a horse how to carry a rider, and follow the rider's instructions, is called 'breaking it in'. When a horse is being broken in, it gets used to a saddle and reins, and all of the other equipment it will wear.

I DON'T BELIEVE IT!

The first known horse races with riders took place 2000 years ago at the Olympic Games in Greece. The men rode bareback – without saddles.

▼ A show-jumper aims to clear a round of fences without knocking any of them over, and without the horse refusing to jump.

90 Many riders love to teach their horses and ponies how to jump, and show-jumping is a very popular sport. At a show-jumping event, or competition, riders are expected to take their horses around a course, jumping over fences on the way, in the fastest possible time. Both horse and rider enjoy the challenge of jumping, and to do it successfully takes real partnership and trust.

91

Horse racing is said to be the sport of kings. All around the world, horses compete in speed competitions, and their owners are rewarded with prize money if they win. Training and keeping a racehorse is very expensive, and riding a racehorse at top speed can be dangerous – but the thrills make it worthwhile for the people who love this sport.

▲ Thoroughbreds are considered the perfect racehorses – fast, light and comfortable to ride.

► During a flag race the rider has to lean over and reach a flag whilst still moving at high speed.

93

Horses can enter competitions where they are tested on the way they can follow the rider's signals and instructions. This is called dressage, and it is a sport that requires plenty of practice and a beautifully turned-out horse and rider. Marks are awarded for presentation, and the horse's or pony's paces and behaviour.

92

Horse and pony riders often meet to take part in games, races and displays, called gymkhanas. Gymkhanas are great places for young riders to meet other horse-lovers, while testing themselves and their riding skills in a variety of competitions.

94

In cross–country competitions a rider and his or her horse or pony must jump over obstacles. These are usually things that you might find in the countryside, such as hedges, ditches and pools of water. Riders are allowed to walk around the course before the competition, so they can look at each jump and decide how they will approach it.

Saddle up!

95 Keeping a horse or pony is a big responsibility. Horses and ponies are herd animals, so they need attention and company. They also need to be kept warm, sheltered and well fed. A farrier needs to tend to their hooves and feet, and a vet needs to give a horse or pony regular worming treatments and vaccinations.

96 Ponies can live outdoors in a field, but only if they have a place to shelter. Many people keep their ponies at a livery stable or yard – a place where many ponies are looked after for a fee. A pony's stable needs to be kept clean and warm, and that means mucking out every day. New bedding needs to be laid and fresh water provided.

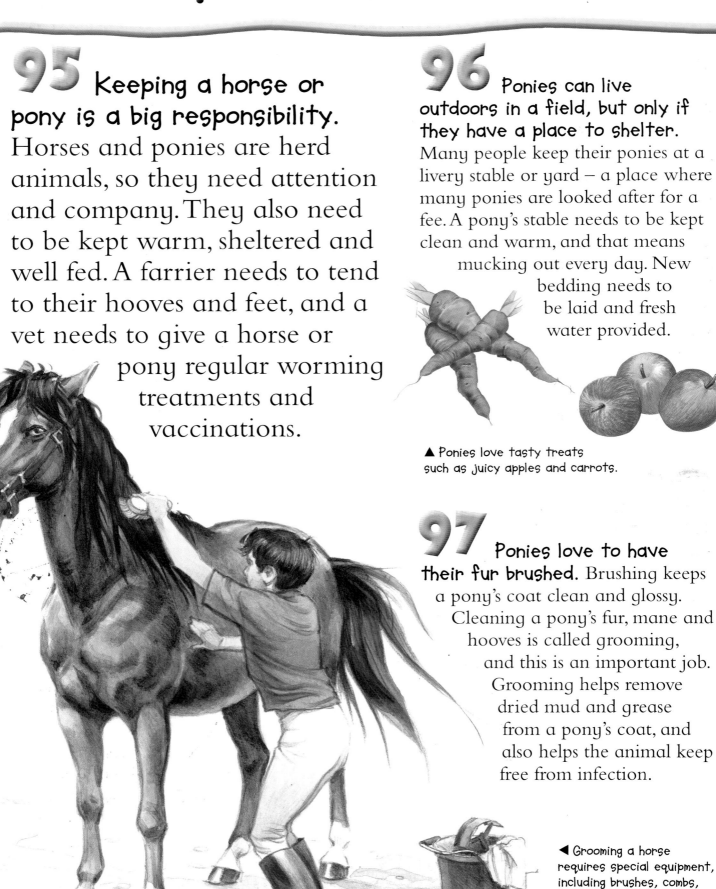

▲ Ponies love tasty treats such as juicy apples and carrots.

97 Ponies love to have their fur brushed. Brushing keeps a pony's coat clean and glossy. Cleaning a pony's fur, mane and hooves is called grooming, and this is an important job. Grooming helps remove dried mud and grease from a pony's coat, and also helps the animal keep free from infection.

◄ Grooming a horse requires special equipment, including brushes, combs, hoof picks, sponges and hoof grease or oil.

2000 years ago an Egyptian queen
saddled an ostrich, and rode it!

98 **Few people can ride without saddles, reins or bridles.** These are all special pieces of equipment – called 'tack' – that make riding easier and more comfortable, for both the rider and the animal! A Russian tribe, called the Sarmatians, are thought to have invented leather saddles in around AD365.

▶ A general-purpose saddle suits most riders, but other types are available for specialist sports, such as racing or jumping.

Cantle
Seat
Girth
Pommel
Skirt
D-ring
Lining
Numnah
Stirrup iron
Stirrup leather

99 **Learning how to ride well can take years of practice.** Riders are taught how to control the horse or pony by using their voices, hands, seat, legs and feet. In this way, a rider can tell the horse to change its pace or direction and to start or stop.

TACKING UP

Only three of these words are real names for part of the tack. Find the fakes!

1. Noseband 2. Nozzlestrap
3. Snaffle bit 4. Smooch lip
5. Throatlash

Answers: 2 and 4 are fakes.

100 **If you don't have your own horse or pony, then riding schools are a great place to learn more and get some hands-on experience.** Riding schools and city farms often welcome interested people who want to learn more about these noble creatures. They also welcome volunteers who are willing to help with jobs such as cleaning the tack, feeding, filling haynets and water buckets, mucking out and grooming the horses and ponies.

Index